D1377393

# G I A N T
# DUMP TRUCKS

Hans Halberstadt

*Motorbooks International*
Publishers & Wholesalers ®

*Dedication*
To my son, Michael Keeler Halberstadt

First published in 1994 by Motorbooks International
Publishers & Wholesalers, PO Box 2, 729 Prospect
Avenue, Osceola, WI 54020 USA

© Hans Halberstadt, 1994

All rights reserved. With the exception of quoting
brief passages for the purpose of review no part of this
publication may be reproduced without prior written
permission from the Publisher

Motorbooks International is a certified trademark,
registered with the United States Patent Office

The information in this book is true and complete
to the best of our knowledge. All recommendations
are made without any guarantee on the part of the
author or Publisher, who also disclaim any liability
incurred in connection with the use of this data or
specific details

We recognize that some words, model names and
designations, for example, mentioned herein are the
property of the trademark holder. We use them for
identification purposes only. This is not an official
publication

Motorbooks International books are also available
at discounts in bulk quantity for industrial or sales-
promotional use. For details write to Special Sales
Manager at the Publisher's address

Library of Congress Cataloging-in-Publication Data
Available

Halberstadt, Hans.
  Giant dump trucks / Hans Halberstadt.
  p.  cm. — (Enthusiast color series)
  Includes index.
  ISBN 0-87938-923-0
  1. Mine haulage. 2. Dump trucks.  I. Title.  II. Series.
  TN341.H35  1994                         94-5338
  622'.66—dc20

**On the front cover:** Earl Hunter is wondering if we're
done with the pictures yet so he can get back to work
with his big Dresser 830E. While he's wondering, you
can glimpse the front tubular frame member by that
left front tire.

**On the frontispiece:** There is about half a million pounds
of dirt in the back of this truck and a little gold mixed in,
too—from about $1,000-$8,000 worth of the precious
yellow metal, depending on how rich the ore is.
*Komatsu Dresser/Haulpak*

**On the title page:** That mass of dirt and rock behind the
truck is about 35ft high and has been freshly fluffed by
the application of large quantities of nitrate/fuel oil
explosive slurry. *Komatsu Dresser/Haulpak*

**On the back cover:** Even though these trucks tip the
scales at about the same weight as a fleet of 100
standard pickup trucks, they accelerate, cruise, and
stop with about the same speeds and agility as
conventional trucks. *Komatsu Dresser/Haulpak*

Printed in Hong Kong

622.66
H157g

# Contents

Acknowledgments ... 6

Introduction **Behind the Wheel** ... 7

Chapter 1 **A Short Course In Mining** ... 11

Chapter 2 **A Short History of Tall Trucks** ... 53

Chapter 3 **WISEDA** ... 71

Chapter 4 **Caterpillar** ... 79

Chapter 5 **Dresser Company** ... 89

Epilogue **Mega Dump Trucks—the Sequel** ... 95

**Index** ... 96

DUERRWAECHTER MEMORIAL LIBRARY
GERMANTOWN, WISCONSIN 53022      SEP 0 4 1997

# Acknowledgments

I am very grateful to three mine operators and three manufacturers, all of whom helped extensively with this book:

Kerr-McGee Coal Corporation, Jacob's Ranch Mine, Wyoming, where Mel Schafer played the role of tour guide and baby sitter.

Echo Bay Minerals Corporation, Battle Mountain, Nevada, Jeff Smith, Mine Superintendent.

Couer-Rochester, Lovelock, Nevada, Tim Maznek, Superintendent.

WISEDA LTD, Baxter Springs, Kansas, where Marilee Hunt, Administrative Services Manager, and Bill Lewis, VP for Engineering, both were generous with their help.

Komatsu Dresser Company, and Sales Support Manager for the Haulpak Division, Bill Bontemps, offered a wealth of support and insights.

Caterpillar, where export sales manager Pete Holman provided an articulate, detailed perspective on the virtues of mechanical drive.

I would also like to express my appreciation to the unsung heroes of the publishing world, the Motorbooks publishing personnel who help me have these adventures and then help clean up the mess afterwards: Tim Parker, Michael Dregni, Greg Field, Michael Dapper, Barbara Harold, Mary LaBarre, Bobbi Jones, Becky Allen, Jana Solberg, and Sharon Gorka. All these folks, in one way or another, are co-authors of my Motorbooks books, and I am grateful to each for their hard work and long hours—for which I, as the author, am unfairly credited.

# Behind the Wheel

We were standing in the chill wind outside the headquarters for Kerr-McGee's huge coal mine about fifty miles south of Gillette, Wyoming, when this *thing,* a big, steel house with a wheel on each corner rolled across the parking lot. I had heard they were big, but I had no idea that anything that big could still roll around on tires.

That was my introduction to the marvelous and mostly invisible world of "mega" dump trucks. It was more than a pleasure—it was a privilege, too, because they don't go out in public; the only time anybody sees them is by invitation and at places like gold and coal mines, far from public roads.

These trucks can, when fully loaded, weigh in at almost a million pounds. They are far too big to be used on highways or roads, too tall to fit under bridges and highway overpasses, too heavy to run on concrete or asphalt without crushing the roadbed. Once you get over the super scale of the things, you see they *are* trucks, and are remarkably like conventional trucks with all the speed and agility of a regular pickup—and about 500 times more hauling capacity.

That first dump truck I saw was a Komatsu-Dresser Company Haulpak 830E, a $2.5 million vehicle that can carry more in a single trip than 500 conventional pickup trucks. Similar ones are made by WISE-DA, Caterpillar, Unit Rig, and the VME division of Volvo, all offering the same kind of upscale efficiency for companies that have to move a LOT of dirt—or gold, silver, iron, phosphate ores, coal, taconite, or all sorts of other raw materials that come from the ground and go into the manufactured goods we buy.

I climbed aboard the Dresser 830 for an inspection. It is a long climb up to the cab, up a ladder like those found on ships. Inside, the cab is extremely conventional:

normal-looking dash, normal-looking wheel, Panasonic cassette player, business-like seats just like you'd find in any conventional truck. But these are very unconventional trucks indeed. From the cab you look down at the road, which is about 15ft below the cab. Remarkably, it drives like a regular truck, too.

Everything about them is big—size, fuel consumption (5gal to the mile), and the cost to buy, operate, and maintain. The sticker price for most 240 ton units begins at about $1,500,000 per truck—and that's for the stripped-down model; bed liners, fancy paint, fog lights, rock-guard fenders, oversized bed, and custom wheels are all extra. Dealer prep and transportation will run you about $25,000 alone. The sheet metal for the floor of the truck bed is 3/4in thick! A *single tire* costs $11,000. If a driver isn't careful, that tire can be destroyed in the first mile of travel. But any incident with these trucks is rare; they are too expensive to drive or maintain at anything less than a very high standard.

These mine haul trucks are so big that the only way to get them from the factory to the buyer is in pieces—lots of pieces. It takes about six semi-truck or railroad flat cars to transport the components of a large-capacity mine haul truck to the mine. Once all the pieces are on site, they are bolted and welded together. The truck will work all day, every day, for about ten years. By then it will have had many new sets of tires, several engine overhauls and replace-

ments, and will have consumed about half a million gallons of diesel fuel. Then, when the warranty period (60,000 hours of operation for the WISEDA trucks) is used up and the when the frame is accumulating cracks and the bearings are becoming worn out, it may be time for the bone yard. But by then each truck will have moved a mountain's worth of material, all by itself.

They come in a range of sizes: *big, bigger, biggest.* The biggest of these off-highway trucks are about 22ft high, 24ft wide, and 43ft long. With a full load in the bed, these weigh in at close to a million pounds, gross vehicle weight (GVW).

And they offer huge benefits to the mine owners. These big trucks actually *save* mine operators money because they can move more material at less cost than smaller vehicles. The result is that they normally operate twenty four hours a day, seven days a week, shuttling back and forth with their cargoes of dirt and coal and gold and silver.

The biggest will be rated to haul 250 tons—half a *million* pounds—of material at 35 mph. That 250 tons might include, for example, over $2,000 worth of gold, or enough coal to heat a whole neighborhood for an entire winter—and will typically move it for about 16 cents a ton. Everything about these trucks and the places where they work is BIG—the trucks, the mines, the economies, the importance of the work these things do. The result is smaller *unit* cost for each cubic yard of material they haul, and lower costs for things like electricity that are generated with the coal they carry. Actually, WISEDA has found some operators overloading these trucks up to 350 tons, but that reduces vehicle life, raises maintenence costs, and can void the warranty.

Even that 250 tons is less than the truck can actually manage; they cut back on the capacity a little to make them last longer. But when WISEDA was building their 240-ton truck, the engineers decided to see how much their new baby could *really* hold, and they filled one up with 270 tons of damp dirt and coal, just to see what would bend or break. Engineers are like that, and it is nice to know when they're loading you up with all that stuff, you aren't going to have the tires pop or the frame break while you're a comin' roun' the mountain.

These huge trucks save money by making each cubic yard or ton of material a little less expensive to move than in smaller trucks. For example, if a mine needs to move 15,000,000 tons of coal, ore, or overburden each year, a 120-ton capacity truck fleet will require *six* vehicles at a production cost of $4,065,000 per year. The big 240-ton-capacity trucks can haul the same fifteen million tons in the same time with just *three* vehicles and a production cost of only $3,000,000. That's over a million dollars saved by the mine operator.

Now, you'd think that a lot of experience behind the wheel of other big trucks would be a requirement for a job driving these things, but that's not the case. All of the mine operators I talked to agreed: *the best candidate for a driver of one of these things is someone who has never driven anything bigger than a pickup or a car.*

They've found that people coming out of other construction driving jobs have bad habits that can't easily be broken. They start the job thinking that they already know what to do. Novice drivers, on the other hand, tend to initially be terrified of the trucks—which is not such a bad idea, all things considered. They quickly get over the terror, become accustomed to the size and space of the vehicle, and rather rapidly are out cruising around the mine without any of the bad habits that might have been learned on semis, for example, or gravel trucks, or any of the large vehicles on the road today.

The training program for drivers is, in fact, the second amazing thing about the vehicles. Within the first week of training, a novice driver will be behind the wheel of a Dresser Company 830E or WESIDA 2450, and by the end of the second week, driving alone and earning a paycheck.

# Chapter 1

# A Short Course In Mining

Raw materials for all our food and manufactured products are either grown or mined. Most of our electrical power and all our natural gas and oil is mined. The costs for these products are kept low by efficient production.

There are two basic types of mining, "shaft" and "open pit." Of the two, the latter is by far the safest, fastest, and most economical. In early days, large open pits such as the famous Kennecott Copper Mines near Ely, Nevada, used railroad gondolas to haul large quantities of ore. The Copper Company built a railroad system in the pits and used dozens of locomotives and hundreds of gondolas to haul material to the crusher, the smelter, and the slag heap.

Opposite page, with the dump body elevated, the top of the lip of this Dresser 830E reaches as high as a window in the fifth story of a building. This truck is depositing overburden—dirt and rock—in the never-ending process of rearranging Wyoming.

But several economic developments have made railroad hauling impractical and prohibitively expensive. The productive life of an open pit mine is now about eight years, much too short a period to justify the time and expense of building a rail system. In addition, current conservation and reclamation practices require that the landscape be returned to its original contours and vegetation. Mine haul trucks have proven to be fast and flexible in removing and then replacing mined material.

As an example, most eastern US states use coal-fired electrical power stations. The coal comes mostly from huge deposits in the West, particularly from the Powder River Basin region south of Gillette, Wyoming, where a seam of clean, low-sulfur coal more than 50ft-thick runs for miles under the prairie. There are twenty five different coal mines in the Powder River area, and just one of them sends six entire train loads of coal east every day.

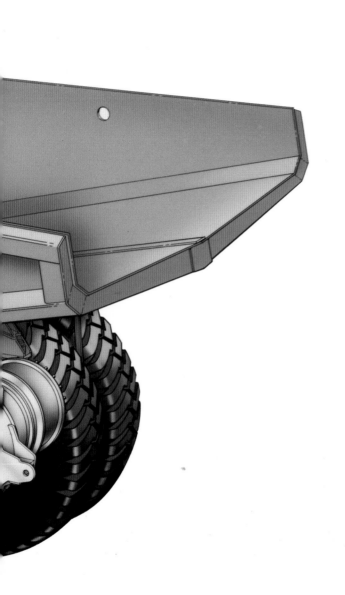

Above, a Dresser 630E. Pretty big, huh? You'd think so, but the big boy in the background isn't even the biggest at this mine; it is only the shrimpy little 190-ton Model 630E. Even so, those "monster" trucks from the car shows better run and hide from this or any other mine haul truck. Any of these could squish a "monster" truck flat—and many people wish they would!

Left, this cutaway drawing illustrates the typical powertrain layout: engine, cooling fan, and electrical controls forward, alternator amidships, and wheel motors housed within the wheel hubs. *Komatsu Dresser/Haulpak*

While the coal is clean and abundant, you don't get to just scoop it up; it is hidden below a layer of rock and dirt about 75-150ft thick—"over-burden" is what miners call it. While it is possible and sometimes practical to burrow through the overburden to reach the coal, a more efficient method uses open pits. Open pit mining begins with removal of the overburden, then the coal, and finally the overburden is replaced and reseeded in a

Above, a way to judge the immense height of a Dresser 630E wheel. Deb Hazlett is just over 5ft tall and tilts the scale at about 100lbs. She hadn't driven a truck or worked with heavy equipment previous to her employment by Kerr-McGee, but that's just fine. In fact, the best candidates for driving jobs with most mines are people without previous truck driving experience—and without the bad habits that come from that experience.

Opposite page, coal is one of the basic cargoes for the big off-highway trucks. This one has a special bed designed specifically for extremely large quantities of material. *Komatsu Dresser/Haulpak*

restoration phase. Within a few months the terrain looks virtually the same as before—although perhaps a bit lower—with the antelope and elk none the wiser.

The Jacobs Ranch Mine, operated by Kerr-McGee, is one of the big coal operations, sending six trains, each with over a hundred carloads, east every day. It has a reserve of 346,000,000 tons of coal under an overburden. that is, on average, about 135ft thick. The coal contains less than a half-percent of sulfur and is only about six percent ash, making it a clean, very low pol-

luting energy source almost ideal for generating electricity. Each pound of this coal produces about 8,700BTUs for turning the turbines that drive the generators that produce the electricity for New York, Boston, Washington DC, and Richmond, Virginia.

Mines like the Jacobs Ranch (and there are twenty five in the Powder River Basin), and the gold and silver mines of Nevada, are fascinating places. Open pit mining is an amazingly clean and tidy process. Mine operators work alongside the Federal Bureau of Land Management (BLM) to assure that the environment is restored to its original contours. The miners remove the gold ore or the coal. Then, following BLM guidelines, they put everything back pretty much where it came from, with native vegetation species planted in the topsoil. In a short time it is virtually impossible to tell that this part of the land has surrendered any of its bounty. The pronghorns and elk are so abundant and so tame in their home on the range at Kerr-McGee's mine that trucks frequently have to wait for the animals to get out of the road.

## Gold in Them Thar Hills

Compared to open pit coal mining, gold, silver, and other mineral mining is a

Above, standing on the edge of an open pit gold mine like this one, the Echo Bay mine near Battle Mountain, Nevada, it's hard to believe that mining only affects one-tenth of one percent of all Nevada's landscape. It is harder to believe—but true—that the productive life span of a mine like this is only about eleven years.

Opposite page, a Cat 789 coming at you. The 789 has been Cat's workhorse, a 190-ton mechanical drive truck that is probably the most popular Cat mine haul truck in the industry—in the world. You'll find them in Russia, Australia, and in many African and South American nations.

Above, there are quiet, comfortable accommodations for two in the spacious, air conditioned cab of this Dresser Haulpak truck. Stuff a cassette into the stereo—Willie Nelson's *On the Road Again* seems appropriate—and get out there and burn up the mine haul highway.

Above, these two trucks—a WISEDA 2450 (right) and a Cat 789—use quite different drivetrains to accomplish pretty much the same thing, although the Cat is smaller, at 195-ton capacity, than the WISEDA. Both are being served by a large Hitachi tracked shovel. Mine owners sometimes will run trucks with identical specs from different manufacturers side-by-side for years to test performance in "real world" conditions.

Below, pressure sensors in the suspension of this WISEDA 2450 measure the exact weight of the material in the truck; at a predetermined load, a system in the truck signals the shovel operator that it is time to go.

very different proposition. Gold in trace amounts is present almost everywhere, but in such small amounts that it is not practical to extract it from the rock in which it is dispersed. Chemical processes have been developed, however, that can efficiently remove even small amounts of gold and silver from large volumes of ore. Combine these processes with the efficiencies offered by large-scale pit mines and mine haul trucks, and ore that was once far too poor to get anyone's attention is now

Opposite page, the efficient operation of a modern mine depends on a carefully calculated interaction between several different kinds of technologies. Without a shovel to match its capacity, the big trucks would be just expensive curiosities. This massive P&H shovel scoops up the equivalent of 100 regular pickup truck loads in every "dipper" cycle. It takes three dipper cycles to fill each truck. *Komatsu Dresser/Haulpak*

Opposite page, loading operations are momentarily suspended while the welder makes repairs to the big 50 cubic yard shovel. The shovel is electrically operated, fed by a 4,160 volt/3-phase extension cord; during "dipper" operations, the system uses current on the up-stroke of the shovel, but it *generates* electricity as the shovel drops back down.

Below, this 190-ton capacity Dresser 630E has an aftermarket bed designed specifically for moving coal. It uses a tailgate and bed side extensions to provide greater volume capacity. Notice the relatively short wheel base; turning radius is only 80ft—not bad at all for a vehicle that is about four stories high and that carries as much as a hundred conventional pickup trucks!

yielding large quantities of mineral wealth.

Mining is one of Nevada's big businesses, even though mines occupy only a tenth of one percent of the state. Even so, each year Nevada produces over $2 *billion* worth of gold and silver—about 180,000 tons of gold and 575,000 tons of silver. Nevada produces 11 percent of the world's gold, and over 60 percent of US gold production.

Mining for gold, silver, taconite, coal, or barite is both simple and complicated. Once you know where the material is buried, the rest is pretty straight-forward.

DUERRWAECHTER MEMORIAL LIBRARY
GERMANTOWN, WISCONSIN 53022

1204

It's a simple matter of: scooping away the waste material; putting it aside for a bit; collecting the coal, gold, or silver ore; then putting the waste material back in place. Complicating things are: the tremendous volumes of waste and ore; the need for efficiency and economy; and the tremendous scale of everything that happens. So while there's gold, silver, and coal just about anywhere you look, the only way you can profitably get at them is to be very, very

Above, part of Kerr-McGee's fleet of heavy Dressers wait patiently for their turn at the scoop. Notice the variety in bed size and configuration among these Dresser 630E and 830Es.

Left, one of the smaller shovels takes a quick maintenance break. That big reel on the right follows the shovel around; it keeps the extension cord tidy and out of the road. Behind the shovel is your electricity in the raw—clean, pure, low-sulfur coal destined for the power plants of the eastern United States.

23

Above, when the dump truck body tilts to discharge it's half a million pounds of gold and silver ore, the lip of the bed is about 45ft above the ground—about as high as a window in the fifth story of an apartment house or office building. This Dresser 630E is delivering ore to a crusher where the rocks will be pulverized, then processed to suck out the gold hidden within. The 630E is a mid-sized diesel-electric with a capacity of 135 cubic yards and a weight of about 170 tons. *Komatsu Dresser/Haulpak*

Opposite page, fifty yards and about 50 tons of material pour into the back of this big 830E. To protect the truck from such shocks, the bottom of the bed is steel plate 3/4in thick and the cab is protected by a canopy built into the body of the dump section. *Komatsu Dresser/Haulpak*

Above, it takes about ten cycles from this Cat 992 wheel loader to fill this Cat 776/777 truck, making each truck cycle far slower than the big 240-ton trucks when they are teamed with 50 yd$^3$ shovels that can fill the bigger trucks with only three to five dipper cycles.

Left, here's a Cat 789 truck at speed in a rare white paint job. One of these vehicles moving at speed is an awesome thought.

Above, most big mines fire a "shot" once a day, normally at a regular time. This shot was fired about a tenth of a second ago. Seven hundred and eighty seven charges, each containing about 300lbs of ammonium nitrate-fuel oil slurry, have just been initiated. The span from left to right in this photo is about 200yd.

Above, that stuff flying several hundred feet into the air is gold ore—several million dollars worth. But it is so diluted that you can't see any evidence of the gold in the ore, and special chemical processes are required to extract it. The little rocks visible are actually huge boulders flying through space. A sense of scale is provided by the two little vehicles on the far right side of the picture—those are both big Caterpillar dozers.

Above, wheel loaders like this Cat 992 wheel loader are mobile and flexible. Cat's line of wheel loaders for mine use range from 3 yd$^3$ to 13 yd$^3$. Here, it's loading a Cat 776/777 truck.

Above, a flock of WISEDA 240-ton "targets" await their turns at the shovel.

Above, one reason they don't send these trucks into town for a trip to the store is that the driver might have a little problem spotting grandma over in the slow lane. Visibility is *quite* restricted, as you can see from the deck of this Dresser 830E. Drivers learn to compensate, partly by becoming very proficient at judging the view in the wide-angle mirror.

efficient. If it weren't for these big trucks, and the savings they offer, mining some ore bodies just wouldn't pan out.

Operation of these mines is based on doing everything with maximum efficiency around the clock and calendar, and it's made possible by the large haul trucks like the Dresser 830Es. Even though the trucks cost millions of dollars each, cost about $120 an hour to run, and are worn out in about ten years, they permit mine operators to move a ton of ore, dirt, or coal for only about 16 cents—about one-third of what it used to cost with smaller, 32-ton trucks.

## It's a Blast

You can't load the coal until you can get at it, and the best way to get at it is with explosives. Most of the waste material—the overburden—is too solid to permit the shovels to scoop it up, so it has to be loos-

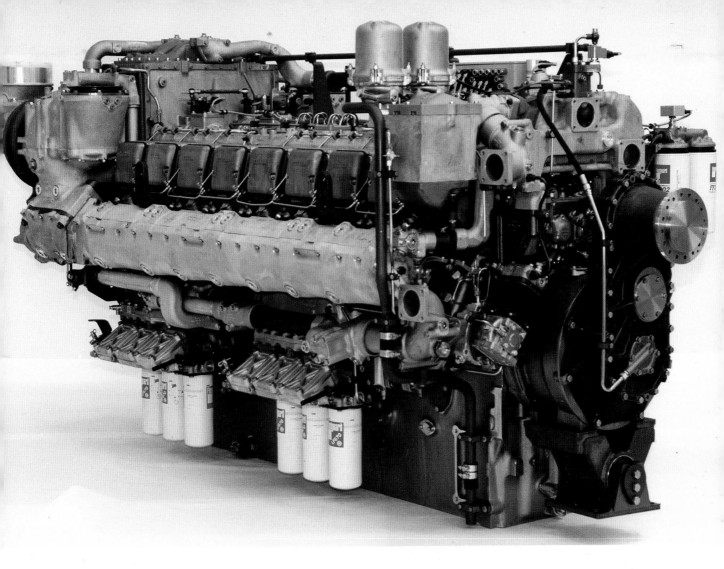

Opposite page, Earl Hunter checks out the massive stern of the flagship of WISEDA's fleet, a WISEDA 2450. Although the basic layout of each of the 240-ton trucks is basically the same—two axles, dual tires on the back, about the same size, shape, and general conformance—note that WISEDA's rear end is a little less cluttered than other designs, and that the engine exhaust vents under the body near the pivot points rather than coming out of the bed support structure, as with other models.

Above, big trucks get big engines. This one is a V-16 model 396 from the German firm of MTU. Those sixteen cylinders each have a 6.3in bore and 7.1in stroke for a displacement of 63.3 liters, generating 2505hp. Red line is only 1900rpm. The engine alone weighs about the same as five passenger cars, over 11,000lb. MTU has sold 2,500 of these 396 engines, the world's most powerful currently in active service. MTU is now offering a new 595 series engine with 3,200hp for mine haul trucks—double the power of the engines that were considered the leading edge of technology only a few years ago. *MTU North America, Inc.*

Above, the Dresser 630E (slightly distorted here by the wide-angle lens) dwarfs Deb (who's up on the deck)—and everybody else, too. Those tires are 36x51 PRs. The truck is 39ft long and about 25ft high.

Opposite page, the mid-sized Cat 777 is a workhorse for the Couer-Rochester gold mine outside Lovelock, Nevada. That's because the 777, with its mechanical drive train and moderate capacity, fits the size and scale of the way this mine conducts operations.

ened, broken up, and pulverized. That's where the blasters come in. A major part of every mining operation involves the placement and detonation of massive amounts of explosives. Instead of high explosives like dynamite, these mines normally use a slurry composed of ammonium nitrate (a common fertilizer ingredient) and fuel oil. This mixture can only be detonated under certain conditions—it must be confined, and it takes something with the explosive intensity of a blasting cap to reliably prime it.

When it is time for a mine to start working a new "bench," the drilling crew will spend several days boring holes about 6in in diameter, about 35ft deep, 10ft apart over an area that may cover the size of several football fields. The result will be about

Above, another view of the 190-ton Cat 789 at speed. Cat has stayed with the mechanical-drive truck in spite of the claims and marketing successes of the electric-drive builders, and has its own version of just who is king of the lode. According to Cat, the title goes to its best-selling, fuel-efficient, mechanically reliable truck.

800 holes, each of which receives a charge of nitrate/oil slurry. These are then primed, the priming charges all connected to trunk

lines, the trunk lines connected ultimately to a "hell box" (no longer the hand-held generator, today the hell box is a computer system).

Large mines will usually blast once a day, normally at a set time. As the scheduled blast time approaches, all vehicles and miners will be evacuated from the vicinity of the blast. Warnings are transmitted over the

Above, Earl checks the security of the fluid-fill panel on this WISEDA 2450. Although a sheet metal cover provides some protection from dirt and rocks, these critical components are checked for cleanliness and security before each shift.

radio. Supervisors count noses to confirm that everybody is out of danger. The master blaster presses the button, there are five short beeps from the hell box, a pause, then one long beep as the hundreds of blasting caps initiate their charges... and with exquisite slowness, a huge section of the mine rises up into the air. From half a mile away, what seem like small rocks can be seen soaring into space—they are boulders, perhaps 10ft across. The sound of the shot echoes back and forth across the pit for twenty seconds or more, then dies away. Millions of pounds of rock and dirt and gold and silver are now fluffed up, softened, ready for the scoop, the mill, and the refinery.

"North road all clear," comes the radio report to the pit boss as the last of the dust settles.

"Ten-four. Pit Five to all personnel: channel one is clear. You may resume normal pit operations."

Everybody goes back to work. New

access roads are built first. Soon the huge electrical shovels roll up to the new work area. With the help of a few wheeled loaders to keep things tidy, they start to work on the material. The biggest shovel has a scoop that holds over fifty cubic yards of material. Three scoops will load the big 170-ton trucks, and five will load the biggest 240-ton WISEDAs and Dressers. The shovel works continuously, without pause, around the clock. The trucks slide back up into position to await their turn. Three "dipper loads" and each truck is full; with a beep, each rolls off to deliver the load. Without skipping a beat, the shovel turns to fill the truck on the other side while a new truck slips into position where the first had been. In a few days, the entire area will have been worked, and the blasters will be ready for another shot.

The haul trucks deliver the overburden to a previously mined area, where it is deposited. After the overburden is removed, the coal is removed the same way, but delivered to a preparation plant for processing. At the Jacobs Ranch mine this is done at the rate of 4,000 tons per hour. The coal is loaded aboard rail cars and headed east within hours of being mined, and the overburden is back in place as part of the reclamation process that proceeds continuously.

Opposite page, a Dresser 830E is in the shop for a little routine maintenance—well, actually, nothing about the truck is little, even the garage. That massive rear axle is about 5ft in diameter.

Above, the steering gear on this WISEDA 2450 isn't too different from any other truck or car, except in scale. The actual size of the engine seems far too small in proportion to the volume of the vehicle. The truck's tires are routinely chocked whenever the vehicle is parked.

Above, Oh, no! The differential is missing from
this Dresser 830E!!! Actually, it was missing
from the design of these electrical-drive trucks;
there's enough empty space in the rear axle
to climb in and take a nap—but the mechanics
are far too busy and professional to do anything
like that. The access panel allows inspection and
maintenance of the huge GE 787 drive motors
inside the wheel hub from the inboard side.

Above, just leaving the shovel, this big WISEDA 2450 has a full quota of payload. Although ore concentrations vary, there is between 10oz and 25oz of gold in this single truck load—a pound and a half mixed in with a half-million pounds of dirt and rock (and a fair amount of silver, too).

The trucks operate around the clock, in snow, ice, rain, and dust, and most are at fairly high altitude, at or above 5,000ft. They are driven about as fast as a regular pickup truck, about 30mph, even at three in the morning during a blizzard—with drop-offs from the side of the road unprotected by guardrails and with sheer drops of over 1,000ft.

Left, the driver—no shrimp himself—provides a scale to judge the massive 240-ton, a Dresser 830E.

Above, Cat isn't the only builder of large mechanical drive mine haul trucks painted yellow. This marvelous rendering provides an x-ray view of the major systems of this 95-ton truck, a Dresser 33M.

Opposite page bottom, you need a ladder to get into the engine compartment of a Dresser 830E, but there isn't a whole lot to be done once you get up there. One of the things that needs checking, though, are the connections for the ducting that feeds filtered air to the engine air intake. The mechanic provides some scale to judge the size of the cooling fan behind him.

Above, Earl Hunter inspects the engine oil level dipstick on a WISEDA 2450. The WISEDAs have their own built-in ladder to assist entry into the engine compartment. WISEDA offers three *basic* engines for the 2450: a Detroit Diesel V-16 149, a two-stroke-cycle with 1800-, 2000- or 2200hp; a Cummins KTTA-50C or K2000, both four-stroke engines with 1800 or 2000hp; a MTU V-12 396 four-stroke 1850hp. Other, much larger engines are also sometimes installed. MTU is currently offering a 3200hp diesel for use in these trucks—and in the next generation, a 300-plus ton capacity that may be coming down the road any day now.

Above, these huge Goodyear disc brake assemblies are mounted on the outboard portion of the wheel hub assembly. Inspection is easy— and a part of the daily routine.

Left, Earl Hunter, like all other drivers, performs a pre-shift vehicle inspection that is pretty much like a pilot's preflight inspection. Here Earl's checking the big Goodyear 40x57 tires on his WISEDA 2450. They last about 10,000 miles if they're driven carefully, about a mile if they aren't. A single wayward rock can destroy one, and on those extremely rare occasions when they blow, they blow *loud*. According to some tire makers, this is the biggest size that can be shipped by truck or rail to the mine site; tires appear to be the limiting factor preventing larger trucks.

Above, the Cat 777 is powered by a Caterpillar 8-cylinder diesel engine generating 920 gross horsepower at 1750rpm. That's about double the power of diesel engines used in eighteen-wheel semis out on the freeway. The engine uses twin turbos, is fed by a Cat fuel injection system, and has four valves per cylinder; the engine has a 6.7in bore, a 7.5in stroke.

Right, even the pistons in million-dollar engines fail eventually. The skirt section of this one has separated at the lower ring. Such failures are rare—and to be anticipated from engines that run about twenty-two hours a day, seven days a week, for years on end.

Above, another view of Deb's rig, the Dresser 630E, at speed. The 630E is Dresser's 190-200 ton class vehicle with an empty weight of 283,000lb and a MGVW of 685,000lb, only about 150,000lb less than the 630's bigger brother, the 830. Truck 26 has a bed extension that increases the volume capacity of the truck for lighter materials, although the weight restrictions still apply.

Right, even though the engines are huge, the components are not much larger than you'll find in more conventional vehicles—and, as with conventional engines, valves need routine attention.

Above, every one of these trucks is, in a way, a custom vehicle. No, they don't get mag wheels and candy apple paint jobs, but each buyer normally demands a different set of specifications in exchange for their $2.5 million; this one has an unusual ladder arrangement that ought to make it a collector's vehicle someday. *Komatsu Dresser/Haulpak*

Left, notice that Cat 789's rear axle is much smaller than the equivalent electric drive vehicles, and the beefy suspension elements and bed supports. Also visible are the pivot points for the bed and the exhaust outlets; the heat of the exhaust is used to warm the bed of the dump section to keep the load from sticking during extreme cold weather.

Above, Deb Hazlett scurries up the ladder to the cab of her Dresser 630E.

Left, here's what they look like when they're new, all clean and pretty. But this truck works for a living, around the clock, and will soon be spattered with mud, dinged by flying rocks, smudged by exhaust. It should be good for about ten years of continuous service, about 80,000 hours of operation. That little thing at the bottom of the ladder is the driver, not a little kid with a mustache. *Komatsu Dresser/Haulpak*

52

# Chapter 2

# A Short History of Tall Trucks

The design of these trucks is a response to many conditions and criteria. Mines traditionally have been extremely dangerous, dirty, stressful places for people to work. But, like so many other things in mining, these trucks were designed with the motto, "safety first."

The trucks operate around the clock, in snow, ice, rain, and dust, and most are at fairly high altitude, at or above 5,000ft. They are driven about as fast as a regular pickup truck, about 30mph, even at three in the morning during a blizzard—with drop-offs from the side of the road unprotected by guardrails and with sheer drops of over 1,000ft. All these conditions might make for a dangerous work place, but

Opposite page, the traditional layout for dump trucks, six wheels with two forward and four in back, has proved to be the best solution to the problem that anybody has come up with so far. But each of those massive tires costs from $11,000 on up and will last about 40-60,000 miles or less. *Komatsu Dresser/Haulpak*

many features and procedures have been developed to make truck driving in the mines a relatively low-stress, satisfying, and safe occupation.

The first big modern-design trucks designed for use in open pit mines were developed in the late fifties (Haulpak Company claims the first, a mechanical drive, built in 1957) and early sixties (Unit Rig & Equipment Co. made the first diesel-electric drive in 1962). These were mechanical drive vehicles, with conventional engine and powertrain systems much like any other truck on the road, with capacities of 20 or 30 tons at first, growing rapidly to 65 tons within a few years. The mechanical drivetrain—diesel engine, torque converter, mechanical transmission, differential—turned out to be the limiting factor for the vehicles. As the components got bigger, so did the maintenance costs, and the weak link seemed to be the transmission.

The truck designers of that era adapted

Above, despite the size of these trucks, mine traffic is *fast*. The trucks turn laps, rather like race cars; the speeds are only in the 30 to 35mph range, but that is plenty fast for the grand prix de Wyoming where the gold medal is in the back of every truck, a new one on every lap—production, efficiency, profitability, lower prices for consumers. One of the ways drivers are evaluated is on how many laps they turn in a shift. A Dresser 630E is shown barreling along here.

the same basic technology used in diesel locomotives: a large engine coupled to an electrical generator instead of a transmission, the generator, in turn, wired to powerful wheel motors. The first of the breed were introduced in 1963, with a capacity of 85 tons, and just two years later the first 100-ton capacity truck hit the road. The result for mine operators was a sudden and dramatic decrease in maintenance costs and a huge increase in truck availability.

It was obvious that increased capacity meant higher efficiency, but it took time to figure out how to make these trucks even larger. By the late sixties their capacity had grown to 120 tons, then to 150 tons by 1970. About twenty years ago the first 170 ton diesel-electric truck was introduced; WISEDA built the first 200+ton diesel elec-

Above, this Dresser 630E is taking on a load of overburden, the simple dirt that covers the Powder River Basin coal deposit to an average depth of about 75ft. When the shovel operator decides, based on experience and judgment, that it is time to go, one blast on the shovel's air horn will send the driver off on another trip across the bench.

tric rear dump hauler in 1982, and today the standard of the industry is the 240ton truck. And although the diesel-electric technology has come to dominate the market, Caterpillar today sells a 240-ton capacity truck with a mechanical drivetrain.

Those 170-ton trucks have turned out to be the workhorses of the open mine industry, and can be seen zipping around most coal, gold, silver, and other mines in the US, Canada, and elsewhere around the world. But, as big as they were, they *still* weren't quite big enough for some mine operators, and 200-ton designs were built and tested as far back as 1970. These early "mega trucks" used power packs and drivetrain technologies borrowed directly from railroad locomotives—and they didn't work out. The diesel engines had the horsepower but were designed for low RPMs and were extremely heavy. The electrical drive motors were also exceedingly heavy and didn't match the requirements of a truck, even one on steroids.

There are four essentials to building any successful vehicle: chassis, drivetrain, tires, and powerplant. For these big trucks, the critical component became a diesel engine with sufficient power—2,000-2,500hp for the biggest models today—*and* relatively high RPMs and throttle response.

Dead weight on a mine haul truck costs about $2 per pound per year, so the chassis needs to be a compromise between strength and light weight. Originally, mine trucks were built according to the "one pound of truck equals one pound of payload" theory, although the new ones are about 1.4lb of payload to each pound of truck. Light weight reduces stress on the tires and allows the trucks to climb the fairly steep grades found in pit mines.

The general layout for these trucks is approximately the same, regardless of man-

Below, while the Dresser 630E maneuvers into position at the shovel, a "blade" attends to the housekeeping chores, cleaning up spills and keeping the haul road clean and neat.

Above, Kerr-McGee's Dresser 630E Number 2026 is powered by an 1800hp turbocharged diesel engine driving a GE GTA-22 alternator connected to two GE 788 wheel motors. Dresser and WISEDA both claim that electric-drive technology is, when you get to the bottom line, the most economical method. Caterpillar, though, has stuck with mechanical-drivetrain technology—for which it also makes a strong claim for high efficiency.

ufacturer. The chassis is designed so that the weight is distributed about equally on the front and rear tires when empty (there are normally two wheels forward and four wheels aft); loaded weight distribution shifts about two-thirds to the back axle, one-third on the front, all in an effort to load all tires equally.

## Frame and Suspension

The frame is built up from sheet nickel-copper (WISEDA uses A710 alloy steel, a particularly costly but tough and flexible formulation, and other builders use similar alloys), welded together in what the builders call a "donut" or "horse-collar" frame, with tubular cross-members. This particular type of alloy resists cracking when cold, a problem with other materials and a cause for the failure of some earlier designs. The frames from all builders tend to be somewhat wedge-shaped when viewed from the side, with lots of material in the rear to support the loaded bed. The "horse collar" surrounds the engine, adding stiffness to the front end of the structure.

The frame is an extremely critical part of these vehicles, even more critical than those of cars or conventional trucks because of the loads and stresses placed on these haulers. The manufacturers have all pretty much converted to using computer-aided-design (CAD) and -manufacturing (CAM), and you can see why. One of the builders, Dresser Company, also puts the frames and other major components through a testing program that flexes and stresses these components in a lab environment, looking for weaknesses in design and construction before the trucks are shipped.

One novel feature of these big trucks has been the use of engine exhaust gasses to heat the vehicle dump body, making the steel alloy less susceptible to cracking on frigid Nevada and Wyoming winter nights and to keep the load from freezing to the bed of the truck. The exhaust is ducted into the frame from the engine, then vented at the back; designers, though, are moving away from this system because the exhaust

gases erode the metal passages over time.

Another novel feature is that the engines, and many of the other components, are designed for relatively easy removal and replacement. The engine usually is mounted on rails that allow the power pack to slide forward, out of the truck, for easy access and major maintenance. For smaller chores, though, a ladder is required because the upper portion of the engine is about 10ft off the ground.

The suspension systems are somewhat similar to those of conventional vehicles, hydro-pneumatic designs, but much larger and with some modifications. Good handling and ride are just as important in a mine truck as any other professionally driven vehicle. Instead of gas/oil shocks, some trucks use solid rubber components to replace shock absorbers and springs. The huge rear axle is actually a tube that supports the rear drive motors and wheel hubs. The rear axle is attached to the body with drag links and "elastometer" rubber suspension elements that transmit the load from the frame to the wheels.

The front wheels and steering gear aren't too different from those on smaller vehicles. While the specs vary a bit from one make and model to another, a typical 240-ton WISEDA truck's front end has 1 degree of camber, 8 degrees of king pin inclination, and 4 degrees of caster angle; the result of this design is that the vehicle has a tendency to return to a straight-ahead direction. This WISEDA design's wheels maintain their positive camber as they move vertically. Steering forces tend to self-cancel. The result is a vehicle that minimizes wear on the tires and the driver.

Some trucks use massive versions of conventional nitrogen gas-over-oil shock absorbers while older WISEDA models employ a Firestone product called a "marshmallow," a rubber cushion and guide assembly that appeared to do the same thing with no moving parts at a lower initial cost and with minimal maintenance; WISEDA stopped using the product recently though because it turned out to be less economical in the field than nitrogen/oil shocks. The front wheels have a full 12in of vertical travel. These front wheels themselves rotate dual roller bearings fitted to axle spindles that are up to 18in in diameter.

## Drivetrain—diesel-electric

As noted, the idea behind the diesel/electric trucks is essentially the same as that used on railroad locomotives: A very powerful diesel locomotive drives a generator, and the generator's output powers large, geared-down, DC motors at the wheels.

The GE 787 motors are geared down through a planetary gear system, normally at about a 28.8:1 ratio (although higher and lower ratios are available, depending on builder and on buyer). The current to drive these motors is controlled through a large power management system located next to the driver's cab.

Above, this ore body was once mined with traditional methods of shafts and tunnels; the rusty rails that once guided ore cars deep below ground are now exposed to daylight for the first time in many decades. While the scoop and truck work the bench, the drilling crews are busy on a shelf several hundred feet up the pit. *Komatsu Dresser/Haulpak*

When the driver steps on the accelerator, an electronic signal to the engine electronic governor causes the diesel engine to speed up, and that drives the alternator. Electronic controls, regulated by the retard and throttle pedal which each operate a potentiometer cause the engine to speed up. Engine speed is controlled by power demand. With the new GE Statex III system, the micro-processor controller for the drive system looks at power demand and cuts back on engine speed if full horsepower is not required. Direct current is generated, and a set of "power contractors" in the electrical power management

Above, finally, a turn at the shovel for this Dresser 630E. It takes about three 50 cubic yard dipper cycles to fill this 630 to capacity. The shovel operator and the truck drivers never miss a beat; while one truck is being loaded on one side, an empty truck is backing into position on the other. As soon as one is filled it drives away and the shovel starts servicing the other truck, without a break in the tempo.

system are engaged. Current flows to the wheel motors through thick cables about 2in in diameter, and the current turns the motor. It is an elegant system with a minimum of parts—although all the parts are large ones.

## Drivetrain—Mechanical

Smaller trucks from Dresser Company and everything from Cat use a drivetrain based on a variation of the traditional mechanical drivetrain. Cat's 789 starts with a big 1800hp engine coupled to a Caterpillar-designed and -manufactured twin disc torque converter, and a driveshaft that feeds into a planetary power shift transmission. Cat's automatic transmission is electronically controlled and executes shifts up or down based on factory pre-sets that are designed to make the vehicle more efficient than traditional hydraulic-mechanical designs. The planetary power shift transmission and final drive deliver the torque to the wheels. While this is a more complex system than the diesel-electric set-up, it manages to convert more fuel into haul-miles, and Cat emphasizes those savings. The competition, however, claims the mechanical drive costs more to maintain and that incremental improvement in electric drive control systems have negated fuel savings of mechanical drive.

The electric vs. mechanical controveryis an ongoing question in the industry. Recent tests at the Echo Bay mine showed that the diesel-electric WISEDA truck achieved more ton-miles per gallon than the Cat 789B and that, overall, WISEDA trucks were more efficient—while other tests with other electric drive manufacturer's trucks seemed to allude to achieving marginally opposite results.

## Wheels, Tires, and Brakes

Most (not all) of the big haul trucks use the same basic layout, with two wheels forward and duals astern, all the same massive size. The wheel rims alone are typically 57in in diameter and 29in in width on the 240-ton class trucks; that means the tires are each about 12ft in diameter and weigh about 4 tons apiece.

Those tires are the second-largest cost for operators of these big trucks, right after fuel. Standard for the big 220- and 240-ton vehicles is the 40x57 size (in your choice of bias or radial ply), mounted on 29x57 rims.

At $15,000 to $16,000 and up for a tire, it pays to be very careful about them, so drivers are taught to drive smoothly and to avoid running over rocks in the roadway—a common hazard and one that can destroy a brand new tire.

When a tire does blow, everybody knows about it; they are *loud*. And although an unlikely occurance, if it happens while the truck is bopping around a corner at speed or gets up on a berm, with a full load and a high center of gravity (CG), it is quite possible that the whole rig will roll over on its side like an elephant that has tripped and fallen. Tires last for about 40,000 to 60,000 miles in normal service, although a careless driver can destroy one in the first mile. Tires turn out to be the limiting factor on these vehicles—the 40 x 57 size being the biggest currently built that can be shipped by road or rail.

The oversized nature of these trucks provides the brake designers with a mega-sized headache. The trucks operate at the same speeds as smaller vehicles on construction sites—around 20-30mph—but with a GVW approaching a million pounds, the inertia... well, your dinky little drum-and-shoe brakes just aren't going to stop it.

There are two basic kinds of brakes available to the driver, each operated by its own pedal. The first is what is called a "dynamic" retarder system, a way to slow the truck on grades and when preparing to stop; this turns the wheel motors into generators and instead of using current, they convert wheel motion to electrical power. Although other types of vehicles use this concept and store the resulting power for later use, the trucks convert the current into heat, rather like a huge, mobile toaster, through a bank of resistor grids (on the right side of the cab deck on the WISEDAs) exposed to the air. A high-speed blower provides cooling air flow, otherwise the resistor grid would quickly melt. This dynamic retarder system works best in the slow speed ranges of about 7-17mph.

But the retarder doesn't stop the vehicle, it just slows it and converts inertia to heat. To completely stop the vehicle still requires mechanical brakes—the biggest set of disc brakes anywhere. Again, these are quite like those on cars and conventional trucks, scaled up many times. Usually this involves a big disc revolving at wheel speed instead of drive-motor armature speed; both work and both have virtues. A wheel rotor turns at far slower RPMs, has a far larger disc, and has become the preferred type. The disc and associated calipers are mounted on the outboard side of the wheels where they are quite easy to inspect and service. WISEDA tested the brakes on the 2450 by driving it at 20mph down a minus-6 degree slope; with a 240-ton load, the vehicle came to a full stop in 135ft. Society of Automotive Engineers (SAE) and Canadian braking codes require trucks to successfully perform a series of complete full-brake stops with less than fifteen minutes between stops within a speci-

fied distance. For the WISEDA KL-2450 that test involved a 250 ton load, 22mph road speed, brought to a full stop in less than 120ft.

## The GE 787 Drive System

The 170-ton capacity design appeared to be the practical upper limit for these vehicles until around 1980, when General Electric developed a more efficient drive motor system, their model 787. This is really a rather fiendish design; the motor actually becomes part of the wheel assembly itself, resulting in a complete system that integrates the motor, reduction gear, wheel, and tire. The 787 is a huge motor, almost 6ft in diameter. This size is actually an advantage, offering structural stiffness and strength advantages over motors with smaller dimensions.

Servicing these motors is surprisingly simple—if you've got the tools. The essential components are inside the rear wheel hub assemblies, so all you have to do to get at the brushes, brakes, and planetary gears that drive the truck is to pop off the rear hub and there it all is, ready for your attention.

Gear ratios vary. The big WISEDA comes with a 28:1 standard, but other builders use 32:1. It really depends on the kind of mine conditions where the truck will be working. A low ratio offers higher speed on flat road segments while a higher ratio makes hill climbing with a full truck easier.

One of the main reasons for putting a speed limiter on the vehicle isn't because the young drivers would be out doing "wheelies" in the dirt, or drag racing in them, but because the armatures and the tires are so big that centrifugal forces could tear them both apart. Excess speed causes heat build-up in the tires, too, and that can cause tread seperation and tire failure. That's why General Electric puts a 2400rpm limit on the drive motor armature; at that speed (about 33-35mph) power is automatically cut out and the dynamic retarder is engaged.

## Power Packs and Cooling

There have been several limiting factors for the size of mine haul dump trucks over the years, and power packs were certainly an early one. Initially, locomotive engines were tried, but they were designed for a completely different kind of operating environment. What was needed was something with the power to push a million-pound vehicle up a grade, that was reasonably responsive, and that offered practical fuel economy. The massive weight of the locomotive engines was one of the critical problems of the early trucks.

Until the early eighties, the largest engine for truck use was 1600hp and that just wasn't sufficient for the operating conditions found in the mines. But since then came 1800hp, 2000hp, and now 2500hp and 3200hp diesels to drive the alternator and provide more than enough power, responsiveness, and fuel economy to make the big trucks very efficient.

The big 2500hp diesels are used in the biggest trucks, but not all that go-power is available. The builders sometimes limit available horsepower to about 2000hp to improve economy and durability of these big, expensive engines, but other models may use the full engine output. Engine speed governors are installed on virtually all off-highway trucks to limit top speed to about 35mph; they could go a lot faster but the hazards from driver error and mechanical failure become prohibitive.

These engines are all turbocharged and fuel-injected diesels, usually in V-16 designs, but some in a V-20 format. These immense engines all have a very high power to weight ratio, and they come from a variety of manufacturers, based on the customer's preference; Cummins, Detroit Diesel, Caterpillar, and the German firm of MTU all contribute engines to the breed.

The cooling system uses a removable-tube radiator and large, low-speed fan combination for maximum efficiency. On the big WISEDA 2450, this fan is about 7ft across and spins at only 690rpm. So what? Well, that low speed reduces parasitic power loss from the cooling system to just 50hp—only about 5 percent of the engine output, and a lot less than the old, smaller, high speed fan previously used on earlier designs that consumed about 10 percent of engine output. Total parasitic loss varies with model and manufacturer but on the WISEDA the fan, air compressor, pumps, air conditioner, and battery-charging system account for about 90hp total.

## The Dump Body and Hydraulic System

The dump body looks like a simple design problem but is actually another place where truck designers fuss and fume with each other about what constitutes "best." All are extremely beefy; the steel plate for the floor is about 3/4in thick, the sides are made of about 3/8in plate.

The body of the dump section is formed into a large box that places the load relatively low, with the center of gravity carefully calculated to keep the vehicle from being any more top heavy than it already is. But when the driver backs into the berm to unload that half-million pounds of ore or overburden, it all needs to slide right out when and where it belongs. Since sometimes this material is wet, or frozen, and perhaps quite sticky, this is also part of the designer's concern.

To deal with these problems, the beds are typically broad, flat, vee-shaped spaces. Loaded, the material is carried low. When the big hydraulic rams are actuated, there is nothing to hang up the dirt, rocks, and gold nuggets and they pour out on command. On Cat trucks the floor slopes forward at a 7.5degree angle, shifting the load forward and down as it is dumped in by the shovel. Cat also uses a V-shaped bottom to the body.

The dump bed is raised by a two-or three-stage cylinder—a 13in first stage and a 9in second stage—pressurized by an approximatly 2400psi hydraulic system powered by a pump driven from the engine accessory section. The bed tilts to about 50degrees, the extended lip (which protects the cab from wayward rocks) will top out about 45ft above the ground.

On the left side of the driver's seat is a lever that controls the dump portion of the body. This control has four positions: RAISE, HOLD, FLOAT, and LOWER. When you back into your "drift," you set the hand brake, shift to neutral, pull up on the lever to the raise position. Hold it there while the bed comes up and all that gold ore pours out into the crushing mill. You can speed up the process by raising engine rpm, but it still takes about 20 seconds for the bed to come to the full-up position. At any time during the raise cycle the driver can stop the extension by lowering the control lever slightly to the HOLD position.

Once the load has been delivered, the control lever is lowered to the full down position, the LOWER position; the bed will cycle back down into position in about 9 to 15 seconds. The FLOAT position is the lowest control lever position and the appropriate position for normal, underway operations.

## The Cab

The operator's cab in these trucks is a little armored cubicle framed in heavy steel beams. That's because almost any accident, including the equivalent of a fender-bender at low speed, will be extremely dangerous. Mine operations have a rich potential for hazard: trucks can roll over (although that's

Above, here's another view of the Cat 992 wheel loader in action. This is Cat's biggest wheel loader; it's design includes a Z-bar linkage that permits tremendous leverage to the bucket, essential for the loader to quickly break material out and deliver it to the truck, which, in this case, is a Cat 776/777.

extremely rare); skid out of control on slick, steep grades; trucks can collide with other vehicles; and (perhaps worst) go over the side of the pit and tumble to the bottom. While the safety record of these vehicles and their drivers is excellent, the designers try to take minimal chances.

But when you climb aboard and slide in behind the wheel, all that attention to safety is invisible. Your throne is completely adjustable up and down, fore and aft. The cab is not just air conditioned, it is pressurized to keep dust out, even when you open the door. It is soundproofed, too, filtering out most of the crashes and roars going on outside.

Instrumentation varies from one builder to the next, but all use extremely high-quality components in the dash. One manufacturer (Dresser Company) uses elaborate and expensive liquid crystal displays and touch-sensitive screens. The result looks like something from an F-15E Strike Eagle; the indicated airspeed will be lower but the basic idea is the same. Others use more conventional instrumentation.

The steering wheel is adjustable, too, for tilt and reach. All the controls are designed to be arrayed logically and comfortably, and most are adjustable to suit the full range of operators.

Above, this 240-ton capacity Dresser 830E truck is equipped with the factory standard equipment dump body, good for moving about 170 cubic yards of material. After its turn as a target for dipper, it will lumber off to unload on the far side of the mine pit. Dump angle is 45deg and the height of the bed lip during the dump is 44ft.

# 'Like Driving Your House Down the Street from an Upstairs Window'

Debbie Zimmerman is just over 5ft tall and weighs in at about 100lb. Like many other drivers of mine haul trucks, she hadn't driven anything much larger than a cowboy-style pickup before she came to work for Kerr-McGee's Jacob's Ranch Mine. You'd think that such inexperience would be a handicap for a fledgling driver, but as noted earlier, that's not the case. Fleet owners and trainers all pretty much agree that you need to start working with these trucks without a lot of bad habits developed from operating other, smaller trucks and vehicles. The best drivers seem to be people who show up with an open mind and a willingness to learn.

"All this was brand new to me," Debbie Zimmerman says of her introduction to the profession of mine haul truck driver. "I had no experience with driving or construction, so everything was somewhat overwhelming—the size, the noise, the tires that were taller than your head, the shovels, the track dozers—everything was just huge. But you ride around with a driver for a while, then they let you drive the vehicle while they ride along to make sure you know what you're doing, that you are safe. Then you are on your own.

"You are scared to death," Debbie says with a laugh of that first time behind the wheel. "I was really nervous. But you get over that quickly—they teach you what to do, show you what to look for, and the help of the other drivers who've been here for years gets you through. The first time I was a *little* panicked, but when the time came to actually drive, you go slowly at first. It was hard to judge distances at first; you can't see what's happening over on the far side of the truck, but you learn to know where the tires are, how to back into the dozer, to pull into the shovel, to look out for rocks. But basically, it is just like driving a car—a car that is two stories high!

"After you are on your own for a while and you notice that you are getting into the shovel correctly, into the dump position correctly, you get an enormous feeling of confidence. This happens after only two or three weeks of driving on your own—you know the basics and you are doing these well. Of course you know you've got much more to learn.

"You have to be very aware of what is going on around you, all the time—the other people on the ground, the vehicles moving around you."

Debbie, like every other driver, starts her shift by getting a bus ride to the truck she shares with three other drivers. In her case, that will be at around midnight, because by preference she works the graveyard shift from midnight until 8 in the morning.

The truck will be chocked and the engine will be shut down, but still warm from the swing shift. It will have been fueled earlier in the day; the 1,000gal tank will last for 24 hours of normal operation. Debbie, like all drivers, inspects the vehicle before she accepts it by conducting a "pre-shift inspection." This is very much like a pilot's preflight inspection, a slow, ritualistic walk around the vehicle looking for anything that might be a hazard to safe operation: cracks in the frame (particularly in the "nose cone" area); all the hinge pins are in place; the rims are secure; no cuts in the tires; no leaks from the hydraulic or fuel lines; no broken or dirty headlights; or any other system that may have failed during the last shift. Then she pulls the chocks from the wheels, stows them in their racks, and climbs up the long ladder to the flight deck of the big Dresser Company 830E Haulpak, climbs into the cockpit, and straps in.

"I adjust the seat—*real important for me*—" says Debbie, who's only 5ft 1in, "and make sure the windows are clean. I adjust the mirrors, honk the horn once as a warning, then I start the engine." Engine starting is, for the driver, just like starting a car; you turn the key to the start position, hold it until the big diesel fires, then release it to its spring-loaded RUN position.

The instrumentation is familiar to anybody who has driven a car, although it is a little more complete. Everything is pretty obvious—and of the highest quality: digital tach and speedometer; engine oil pressure, coolant temperature, air pressure, electrical output, fuel quantity. The ignition switch is labeled MASTER SWITCH, and is over on the upper left side of the panel; the key will be in it when the driver takes over the vehicle. In the same part of the panel, right where the driver can easily monitor them, are some of the warning system lights: control air, body up, retard control, lube pressure. On the right side are more warning lights: engine fault, engine check, electrical fault, warm air flow, ground fault, steering pressure, and brake pressure. There are also controls for the retard regulator, the parking brake, head lights, dash lights. Overhead will be the engine hour meter, breaker panel, and a vacuum system control—along with an absolute essential for all truck drivers everywhere, the stereo sound system.

The steering wheel looks like any other, and below, right where they belong, are the three pedals we all know and love—except that two of the three are nothing like their automotive counterparts. The center pedal, the one where the brake goes in a car or conventional truck, is the retarder control; you apply it to slow the vehicle when descending a grade or coming to a stop. The far left pedal, the one that ought to be a clutch, operates the disc brakes; but you use those sparingly, at low speed. The rotors are almost 4ft in diameter and could rapidly heat up to a bright, glowing red if they were to be used indiscriminately.

"It starts just like a car," Debbie says, "and it will usually fire right up. It has a high-idle switch that kicks it up to 1600rpm for a few moments while the air pressure and hydraulic pressure come up." Then the parking brake is released, the gear lever advanced to FORWARD and off she goes for another day in the coal mines.

Mine traffic is almost invariably on the left, British-style. The rationale for that is that, in the unlikely event of two fully loaded haul trucks having a head-on collision (it hasn't ever happened), the chances of the drivers being in the middle of the mix-up are lower; they will tend to be on the outside of the massive ball of twisted wreckage instead of at its center. "If a collision should ever happen," Debbie says, "you will be off-side to off-side, rather than cab-to-cab. This should make it more likely that the drivers will not be directly involved.

"Learning to back into the shovel is very hard to learn. Every shovel operator has a set of peculiarities and preferences, and we have to learn what they are. Some want you to back in quickly, another will want you at a tighter angle, or closer than another, and you learn that by working with that operator." Ideally, the shovel operator never misses a beat; there is always a fresh truck waiting in position on the off side when another truck is loaded and departs. That kind of efficiency only happens when the shovel operator and the truck drivers are fully proficient and are playing on the same team. It is a pretty thing to watch—trucks slide into their positions alongside the vast shovel, are loaded, and depart as fresh trucks arrive in a massive, mechanical ballet.

"*Everybody* works together here," Debbie says. "If there is a problem—a truck blows a tire, for example—everybody knows what to do to cover that problem and to keep things moving efficiently."

Many trucks are equipped with on-board weighing systems that actually measure the weight of the load as the truck is filled. The driver gets a digital display and the shovel operator sees a set of lights—green, amber, and red. When the amber light shows, the truck will take one more bucket of material. These systems are quite accurate, to less than 5 percent. They avoid excessive weights because that over-stresses tires, drive motors, and the frame. And some materials are heavier per cubic yard than others; experience counts here. And when the shovel operator honks the horn, you're full and it is time to go.

"The 830s are so stable that you can't get one to slide," Debbie says. "They will lumber a bit, and if they are heavily loaded they might sink into the roadway a bit, if it is wet, but that's about all. The 830s are *wonderful, wonderful* trucks! They are absolutely marvelous, for being that big—they ride like a Cadillac. They are great trucks! We are *spoiled*."

When the rain or snow turns the road to mud and the wheels start to slip and slide, it only takes a call from one driver to get the whole fleet to pull to the side of the road while a load of gravel is imported to the slick spot for improved traction.

# Chapter 3

# WISEDA

Unless you are in the mining business you probably have never heard of the WISEDA company, but it is a small firm that is a big player in the market for really big trucks. It pioneered the 240-ton design back in 1982, and has offered a lot of innovations before and since.

The company was founded only in 1980 by William S. Davis who had previously been a part-owner of another off-highway truck manufacturer; he and his family still own it. Davis worked for other mine truck builders, thought he had a better way of doing things, and set up shop with some other veterans of the industry. He bought out the assets of a defunct truck builder and set out to build a bigger, better mousetrap, built on the experience of Davis

Opposite page, the four big discs that look like they might be headlights are actually air cleaner intakes on this WISEDA 2450. Dust is a significant problem in the mines, even though water trucks routinely sprinkle the roads to keep it under control.

and the veteran designers he recruited for the new company. Davis's company rapidly became a dominant force in the business.

Davis's interest in a new and larger design coincided with General Electric's development of the 787 drive motor and alternator system. One of the key players, WISEDA's current Vice President of Engineering, Bill Lewis, explains: "WISEDA believed that a larger hauler could be built that would provide the same economies of scale that we had when we moved from 85-ton to 100-ton, from 120 to 150, to 170, to 190-ton. The critical components were there: tires, engines, drive system—all were available. It turned out to be, as we thought, the next generation of truck size, that the economies of scale were there. The truck is now the 'bread-and-butter' size of the industry.

"The electric drive truck does a better job of 'loading' the engine, preventing some of the mechanical shock effects you get with a mechanical drive truck. We are

Opposite page, the top of the bed extension reaches about 50ft from the ground during dumping of this WISEDA 2450. Dump angle is 50deg; it takes 24sec for the body to fully tilt up, powered by two three-stage hydraulic cylinders under 2400psi.

Above, ready to be serviced by the big Hitachi loader, this massive 2450 "King of the Lode" waits for half a million pounds of gold ore. WISEDA ships these trucks all over the world—in pieces.

seeing 18-20,000 hours of operation before overhaul; Caterpillar is looking at 10-12,000 hours before overhaul. The total operating costs in dollars-per-operating-hour are *quite* a bit lower with an electric drive than a mechanical drive truck."

According to WISEDA, component life expectancy for the mechanical-drive Cats is a lot shorter than the electric-drive tech-nology; Caterpillar, on the other hand, has a different perspective.

WISEDA now builds its trucks in a facility at Baxter Springs, Kansas. Each is essentially a custom truck, based on a standard design, assembled to the specifications of the particular mine. While other manufacturers offer a wide range of designs and capacities, WISEDA specializes in the very

Above, you can't get much more material aboard. Even those big tires are showing the effect of the load. This WISEDA is jamming along at about 30mph.

Left, the ore is nicely pulverized by the application of explosives, making it easy for the shovel to scoop it up and deposit it aboard this WISEDA truck.

largest, 220- and 240-ton designs, and only sells diesel-electric-powered vehicles.

One of the major problems for trucks of this type is cracking of frame elements, a result of the tremendous stresses that are inflicted on the vehicle when 50 cubic yards of rock and dirt are dumped into the bed, or when the truck negotiates the twists and turns of a mine haul road. These stresses invariably destroy frames over time, and all builders adopt special steels and strong designs to cope. WISEDA's solution puts extra steel into the frame itself, about 25 percent more than some competing haul

trucks. For the KL-2450, that works out to about 12 percent of the total weight of the truck invested in the frame, compared to 9 percent in other large haul trucks.

WISEDA has a very strict quality control program that documents all the materials used, right down to details like who did the welding and how much welding rod or wire was used. Heat treatment of the frame is measured and documented, then inspected with ultrasonic devices to very strict standards. WISEDA can pull up this kind of history for any truck they've built. As a result, WISEDA warrants the frame for 60,000 operating hours or ten years, the longest in the industry.

Opposite page, in a view that's slightly distorted by a wide-angle lens, it's apparent that the right front tire is a long way from the driver's seat, and one of the things new drivers have a hard time with is judging where that tire is.

Above, tucked into the shovel, this tidy 2450's driver waits for the shovel operator to dump a load aboard. While he's waiting, you can get a peek at the steering gear and suspension.

# Chapter 4

# Caterpillar

The Caterpillar company has been the dominant force in construction equipment for many years and today sells a wide variety of mine trucks, loaders, scrapers, and hydraulic shovels.

Caterpillar and Dresser Company share the same hometown today, Peoria, Illinois, and were both born in the same, sleepy little California farm town many years ago. That town was Stockton, and the forerunners of the Caterpillar company set up shop here in the late 1800s. There were two companies at first, Holt Brothers and the Best Manufacturing Company; they merged in 1925 to form the Caterpillar Tractor Company. Holt already owned a plant in Peoria and after Caterpillar Tractor was formed and manufacture of construc-

The workhorse Cat 789 returns to the loader for yet another lap in the daily productivity race. Mechanical-drive trucks like this one are generally supposed to excel where mine road grades are moderate, and can be less efficient where the roads are steep.

tion equipment was consolidated there, where it remains—just up the street from another migrant from Stockton, the Komatsu Dresser Company.

While Dresser Company and Unit Rig WISEDA were developing the diesel-electric-drive technology, Cat experimented with electric drive trucks in the sixties and seventies but stuck with the tried-and-true mechanical drivetrain. It uses that technology on all its trucks today, including five models with capacities from 35-240 tons. One of Cat's selling points for these vehicles, and for mechanical drive in general, is that fuel economy is better than diesel-electric.

Cat builds just about all its own components, including engines. For the biggest Cat, the 793, the engine is an 1800hp four-stroke turbocharged V-16 diesel with a 6.7in bore and 7.5in stroke (4211ci displacement). The pistons are fabricated from an aluminum alloy; they use three rings and are oil-spray cooled.

Above, the tires on the smaller trucks last only about 5,000 miles, compared to 7,500 or more for the bigger rigs.

Right, this Cat 777 gives us a peek under its fender at the massive brackets that attach the suspension components to the frame.

Cat's frame design is much more box-like than those of other manufacturers, with huge rectangular beams and cross-members. The 789's frame uses two forgings and twenty castings for extra strength at the brackets for the front strut mount, rear suspension pivots, and the hoist cylinder pivot points.

Cat's globe-hopping senior salesman, Gene Holman, describes the line-up: "We make six models of truck, from 35- to 240-ton capacity. We introduced the 35-ton truck to the market in 1963, the 50-ton in 1970, six years later we introduced the 85-ton truck, then in 1985 the 150-ton truck, then in 1987 we co-introduced the 195, then in 1991 we started shipping the 240-ton truck. We used to be in construction

A clean, tidy, and apparently low-mileage Cat 789 awaits its turn for the attentions of the wheel loader. One of the virtues of these somewhat smaller trucks (small only when compared to the 240-ton rigs) is that they work with existing scoops, shovels, and loaders—unlike the big boys that require monster shovels to be at all efficient.

trucks for use on dams, then our 35- and 50-ton trucks started getting used on smaller eastern coal mines. Then, with the 85-ton, we started to move into some gold mines. When we brought out the 150 in 1985, that

Opposite page, that's about 12 cubic yards of gold ore pouring out of the Cat 992 wheel loader into the bed of this Cat 776/777 truck. If you could get at that gold—and you can't, because it is in microscopic particles—it would be worth approximately $100. In fact, this ore would have been considered virtually worthless during the Nevada gold rush years, and the costs of extracting the gold was more than the gold itself was worth until fairly recently. Even though gold prices are far lower than about ten years ago, mining efficiency is far higher—thanks in part to trucks like the Cat, along with the products of Dresser and WISEDA.

Opposite page top, the Cat 777 seems to be jamming right along but its rated cruise speed is no higher than trucks twice as big. That's about 30-35mph under the very best of conditions. But speed really is important; when coupled with safety, it represents higher production and bigger profits.

Opposite page bottom, this particular gold mine has used the Cat 777 tractor, normally supplied without dump body, and converted it to what is essentially a Cat model 777B. This truck is one of the smallest you'll find in the mines, with a gross vehicle weight of only 324,000lbs and a capacity of about 90 tons.

Above, despite the camouflage paint job, this isn't a Dresser in drag, but a mechanical-drive, 190-ton Caterpillar 789 truck, waiting its turn under the shovel. A wayward boulder seems to have scored a hit on the railing surrounding the cab. The body of the truck shows a lot of additional impacts, an unavoidable part of the program for mine haul trucks. Even so, the paint is fresh and neat; these trucks all get plenty of attention to the mechanical and cosmetic details.

was strictly a world class mine truck.

"The thing that makes us different from the other manufacturers is that we build essentially 100 percent of our trucks—the engine, the transmission, the drivetrain, the hydraulics—all of those are ours. Our competitors might make the frame and a couple of other major components, but they buy maybe 70 percent of each truck. These components are essentially out of their control. We at Cat control our components—that's a policy and a strategy.

"We are the world's only mechanical drive truck in the 150-, 190-, and 240-ton class. I've been around the electrical drive system since the sixties—and I think it is a pretty good system—but there are some inherent weaknesses to the system. The first one is that it has a single-speed transmission dictated by the final drive gear ratio. You are locked into a high- or a low-gear ratio. Cat trucks each come with six gear ratios; the driver can change the powertrain ratio. It boils down to what we call *powertrain efficiency*. All the engine horsepower rating tells you is how much fuel you can burn! The *only* horsepower rating that is important is the horsepower at the bottom of the tire on that rear axle.

"If you know the weight of the vehicle, the input horsepower, the grade, and the speed on that grade, you can calculate bottom-of-the-tire horsepower. You can calculate the efficiency of the truck by comparing the input hp with the tire hp—and for Caterpillar trucks, on a 0 to 15 percent grade, we'll put about 85 percent of that input power to the ground. Electric drive trucks will typically be about 72 percent. This means that we can move material at a lower fuel cost per ton of material moved."

Cat also makes some other interesting

Opposite page, detail of the Cat 777 left front. This comparatively small truck only carries about one-third the load of the big trucks, but that works out just fine for some operation, like the Couer-Rochester gold mine.

claims. One is that an operator only really needs one kind of maintenance technician, mechanics. Electric-drive trucks need mechanics *and* electronic technicians. "We tend to run on fewer hours of maintenance than electric-drive," Holman says. "There are about 8,500 hours in a year, and we have Cat trucks that consistently run 7,000-7,400 hours a year; that is *very* difficult to do with electric-drive trucks."

Cat uses oil-cooled disc brakes on all four corners. Other builders use disc brakes in combination with retarders. Even so, Cat's Gene Holman claims its braking system absorbs horsepower with the efficiency of a Formula 1 race car. "We can de-accelerate an 830,000lb vehicle from 30mph in *seventy five feet*! You can't do that with an electric-drive truck; they take from 120-150ft under the same conditions.

"In a way," Gene says, "the cycle times for these trucks are similar to lap times for a race car; your cycle or lap times are somewhat dependent on how comfortable that driver is about 'hanging it out.' Some of these mine haul drivers have been doing this for twenty or twenty-five years. They are incredibly sensitive to the vehicle and the way it behaves on a mine road. If they feel safe, they are going to perform at a higher level than if they are not."

# Chapter 5

# Dresser Company

Dresser Company's ancestry in the construction trades goes back to 1922 and a land-leveling project near Stockton, California. That's when a gent named R. G. LeTourneau developed a new, improved version of the scraper. Scrapers have been around for centuries, both horse- and man-powered, and by 1922 the basic design had been adapted by many manufacturers for use with trucks and tractors. LeTourneau's version was stronger, based on a welded frame, and was much more efficient than previous models. He formed a company to sell the design, the R. G. LeTourneau Company.

LeTourneau motorized the scraper the next year, another innovation. Stockton must have been the approximate center of the construction equipment industry about that time, because Caterpillar was also started in the same little agricultural town (although much earlier), and there must have been quite a bit of cross-fertilization among the engineers and mechanics working in the plants. Both companies departed Stockton for Peoria, Illinois, so their descendants still work in the same community—perhaps accounting for the lively and innovative tradition of competition between the two firms that continues today.

The R. G. LeTourneau Company was absorbed into the Westinghouse Air Brake Company, (WABCO), and the Haulpak truck division was sold to Dresser Company Construction and Mining Equipment Company in 1984. Dresser Company and the Japanese firm of Komatsu Ltd. set up a joint-venture in 1988, the current company called Komatsu Dresser Company—the

Opposite page, the size of truck that will work best in a particular mine will depend on many factors; bigger is not always better, and sometimes the biggest trucks are just too big. This one has a capacity of 200 tons, or about 80 percent of the largest currently available. Even so, this Dresser Haulpak 685E tips the scales at about 250,000lb empty; it stands 21ft high and is almost 24ft across. *Komatsu Dresser/Haulpak*

Above, here comes Kerr-McGee's No. 2030, a Dresser 630E with the Hi-Vol aftermarket bed. Just think, if somebody would just build a cab-over camper for these things, you could have a "land yacht" that could include its own garden.

Left, here comes another 50 tons of overburden into the bed of this Dresser 630E. When the scoop unloads, the whole truck wallows under the impact of 50 tons or so, dropping into the back.

world's second-largest builder of heavy construction equipment.

The important name to remember in all this is *Haulpak*—a name that goes back to the first pioneer of the breed, way back in 1957. That's when WABCO introduced the very first rough, tough, high-capacity construction and mining truck. It was a 32-ton-capacity model—immense for its time—with mechanical drive. That truck revolutionized the business of moving large vol-

Above, here's another view of the Phillipi-Hagenbuch "Hi-Vol" custom body, in this case on a Dresser 630E. Higher bed walls plus a tailgate allow more coal to be carried.

umes of dirt, rock, and ore, made the whole business far more economical that before.

The first diesel-electric drive truck wore a "Haulpak" label, too. That truck rolled out of the factory in 1964. It didn't eliminate the mechanical-drive technology from the industry—Haulpak still sells three models of that type—but it made possible the much larger vehicles that have developed over the intervening thirty years. Over 17,000 Haulpaks have been sold. The Komatsu Dresser Company claims that there are more 100-ton and above Haulpaks in the mines than any competing make (mechanical or electric), and that Haulpaks have the lowest cost-per-ton for ownership and operation in the off-highway rear-dump truck market.

Regardless of the corporate name, the Haulpak division has made some important innovations over the years. Besides that first 32-ton truck and its diesel-electric drive descendant, Haulpak claims parentage to the two-axle, compact, tight-turning design for these big trucks. They also introduced the idea of using exhaust to heat the frame and the dump body to reduce cracking in cold weather; the deep-V shape to

| Cost Per Hour (prorated) | 830E Haulpak | 793 Cat | MT4000 Unit Rig |
|---|---|---|---|
| Preventive maintenance | $1.97 | $3.36 | $2.17 |
| Engine overhaul | $6.24 | $6.61 | $6.46 |
| Engine-Programmed Maintenance | $1.20 | $1.59 | $1.24 |
| Drive System Maintenance & Overhaul | $5.13 | $10.35 | $5.13 |
| Spindles, Suspensions, Hydraulic Cylinders | $2.21 | $2.33 | $5.45 |
| Brake System | $1.84 | $2.58 | $2.10 |
| Other Repairs | $8.78 | $9.25 | $11.74 |
| Tire Maintenance | $25.92 | $25.22 | $25.40 |
| Dump Body Maintenance. | $1.67 | $1.83 | $2.01 |
| Fuel & Lube | $41.82 | $35.81 | $40.45 |
| Driver | $22.50 | $22.50 | $22.50 |
| Total Operating Cost Per Hour | $119.28 | $121.43 | $124.65 |
| Production Per Hour | 756.1 tons | 719.8 tons | 706.9 tons |

lower center-of-gravity; the big, round, extremely strong "horse-collar" frame; a specialized nitrogen-over-oil suspension system; and more recently a computer-driven Haulpack Management System (HMS).

The current line-up of Haulpak trucks range from the (comparatively) puny 140M, a 40-ton mechanical drive truck, to the 830E 240-ton diesel-electric. There are three mechanical-drive models and five electrics.

The Codelco Company operates one of the world's largest mining truck fleets at its Chuquicamata, Chile, mine. Based on actual productivity measurements at the mine, and using typical US operating costs, the company did an operating cost comparison on the 830E, Cat's 793B, and the MT4000, all 240-ton mining trucks, in May of 1993, with representatives from each company observing and verifying the tests. The results, which are shown here, were a bit surprising.

The Cat 793B is a mechanical-drive truck while the other two use diesel-electric

There is plenty of room around the shovel, and on most haul roads, for maneuvering. You drive trucks like this Dresser 830E British-style, though, on the left. Although the roads are dirt, they are smooth and free of rocks—kept that way by a fleet of "blades" that constantly scurry around, keeping the streets clean. That's because a single rock falling off a truck can destroy a brand new $11,000 tire on a following vehicle if the driver doesn't see, or can't avoid, hitting it.

drive. The Cat had about an 8 percent fuel economy advantage as a result, but when the other cost elements were all calculated,

Above, the 630E and the bigger 830E can sometimes be difficult to tell apart, but one helpful breed characteristic is the front wheel hubs—they are a smooth, sheet metal cover on the smaller 630 truck, a ribbed casting on the larger 830.

This side view of the biggest Dresser shows the exhaust ports at the rear of the bed, part of the same type of system used by most mine haul truck builders to prevent cold-stress cracking during extreme weather conditions. You also get an idea of how the truck's designers built in protection for the cab compartment and the fore end of the truck from flying, falling objects like boulders— an occupational hazard for these vehicles.

those saving were offset by higher costs elsewhere. These results were based on a fairly short test period and might not be an accurate predictor of long-term, real world costs, but the test was at least based on vehicles with identical specifications, all operated in the same mine, on the same roads, hauling the same material. The mine is conducting a long-term test, the results of which aren't available at this writing.

# Mega Dump Trucks—the Sequel

When the first big mine haul truck was built, thirty years ago, bystanders probably said (the way bystanders always do) that the 35-ton truck was the final word in truck development and that *nothing* bigger would or could possibly ever come down the road. The bystanders have been saying the same thing about the 240-ton truck, too, and they'll tell you that the tires are at their practical upper limit, that nothing bigger can be shipped by truck or train. That conventional wisdom, once again, seems to be wrong.

As Bill Lewis at WISEDA reports, "There are tire manufacturers looking at making tires two sizes larger than presently available, and—depending on the market—we are fifteen to twenty-two months from having larger tires on a larger truck. We believe that will be in the 300- to 350-ton capacity. It will be a six-tire, two axle truck, like the one we have today. The engine is already available from MTU, and Cummins is looking at building one, too. Tires are about two years away. Drivetrain manufacturers are starting to take an active interest. The market interest is there; a number of mine owners have expressed interest in 300-plus ton trucks.

"As today's mine operators become more experienced with these vehicles, and look at not just the direct acquisition cost but what the vehicle will cost over 60,000 hours, the electric-drive truck is the hands-down winner over the mechanical because of parts and maintenance costs."

# Index

Best Manufacturing Company, 79

GE 787 drive motor, 59, 62, 71

GE Statex III, 59

General Electric (GE) engines and drive
   systems, 59, 62

Holt Brothers, 79

Jacobs Ranch Mine, 15-17, 36

Kennecott Copper Mines, 11

R.G. LeTourneau Company, 89

Westinghouse Air Brake Company
   (WABCO), 89-91

**Giant dump trucks:**

Caterpillar trucks and loaders, 55, 60, 73,
   79-87
789, 60
789B, 61, 80
793, 79
793B, 93

Komatsu-Dresser Company trucks, 36, 58,
   60, 89-94
Haulpak 140M, 93
Haulpak 830E, 7-9, 29, 93

WISEDA trucks, 36, 54, 57-61, 71-77
2450, 9, 62, 63
KL-2450, 62, 77